TIDES

RIA UMBRANI

Copyright © Ria Umbrani
All Rights Reserved.

Contents

Contents

Contents

Foreword

As someone who founded and then managed a global language business for over three decades, I am often asked to give my opinion on the work produced by aspiring language professionals. From copy and content to prose and poetry, I have read and commented on hundreds and thousands of pages. Most work is average; some is good and exceptional has usually been a rarity. So, when I sat down to read Ria's poems, I didn't know what to expect.

It was an extremely busy time of the year, with a little too many professional and social commitments lined up. I had thought I would read a few poems every day and then get down to writing the foreword. Unfortunately, I couldn't start when I had intended to, but when I did, I couldn't stop. I read all fifty-one of them, on the trot, and the foreword pretty much wrote itself immediately thereafter. The thoughts and emotions her words evoked couldn't have waited any longer.

It would be hard to find someone who has not succumbed to the temptation of penning a verse or two. I guess we all have, but Ria is different. Poetry for her does not seem to be a thrill. It is simply how she expresses herself and interacts with the world around her. It is almost like she does it on our behalf. No wonder her poems are so relatable while being this effortlessly brilliant. From topics as mundane as the 'Cupboard' to those as esoteric as 'Life is a raincloud' and then everything in between, Ria has explored the world around her both honestly and fearlessly. Her words have the power to transport us back in time, make us want to linger there a little, send us in a bout of reflection, and sometimes, just for a teeny weeny little moment, help us recreate and relive the times we've lost. Ria goes beyond the trappings of the rhyme and plays with rhythm, something that to me is the truest mark of her brilliance.

Be it the young, the old, the seasoned or then well the aspiring, this little book for poems is for everyone. Written from the heart, it is sure to strike a chord. It surely did with me.

Sandeep Nulkar

https://sandeepnulkar.com

Mine Alone

Resounding in my mind, there always exists a thought,

Imagination whisks me away to a scene of the vivid sort,

Afar I drift from the havoc the world has wrought,

Urges for excitement drift far and wide, never to make port.

My urge and I sail past the places with a warm, familiar glow,

Braving through the vast lands of whose existence no one will ever know,

Receiving fleeting sights of soft, joyfully drizzling rain,

And glimpsing gloomy, lone islands which seem to appear again and again.

Never will I stop walking through the mist of uncertainty

In the only place where misfortune cannot follow me.

Early Work

1. The Seaside

I went to the seaside with a friend of mine
I brought sandwiches and carrots; the total was nine
When a seagull perched on my arm, I started to tingle,
And when it flew away, out came the shingle.
The sea is sparkling bright with the evening light
And fish are jumping without fright
The rock pool is clear, my house is very near,
With Mummy fish out with her baby, crying, "Come back,
dear!"
When it's time to get up, the sun's light
Signals the seagulls to take flight.

(Written at age seven)

2. Grandparent

We love you, that's all we know
If you don't feel it, we aren't letting it show
It becomes easy to forget who you are
Though you are eternally our guiding star,
We may shout, let everything rush out
In all of us, sowing doubt
Sometimes reducing you to tears,
A reality in the form of our worst fears
To try and end your lasting sadness,
We stay the bouts of human madness
And extend a comforting word
'Til appreciation you have heard
We may give in to the lure of evil
But we adore you, and always will
We hate to see you in despair;
That thought is awful, beyond repair
Harmony is all that we aspire to
But more than often, we forget that you
Are the one to whom we owe everything
From our thoughts to the memories to which we cling
For years uncountable, rather than your gain,
You saw to it that we were never in pain.

So, wipe away your tears, dry your eyes
Let us all together realise
It's as simple as this: we're your family, your pride
That you are everything to us can never be denied.

3. The 'Nothing'

When I felt like I was nothing,
I held on to what gave me peace
When it felt right, I spilt all my troubles,
And they slid off just like grease.
Not everyone was by my side
Usually, they spread my grief,
But I was true to myself, and, in time,
I had caught my inner thief.
But many a criminal breaks out
And is hard to catch all over,
I tried not to make a big deal about loss
To develop my own protective cover.
We all do have flaws
And the need to explode at those we accuse,
I tried to stick to my own methods
To willingly light the fuse.
I tried things I thought I'd failed at
Who knew that I would be surprised;
Everyone is good at something
Even if it hasn't been realised.
People pushed me out of the crowd
It happened all the time,

But here's the thing, if you don't expect a fair life
It will feel less like a crime.
I did what I felt was right
As I wanted, I 'd indulge or hide,
Not one person understood
Who I really was inside.
I made the night my refuge
When no one could change my mind,
I pondered and dreamt of wishes come true
People will change, you'll find.

4. Music

How pleasant and sweet
Is a mesmerising tune
It is the day's pleasure
By the light of the moon
To listen and to learn
The melody, its soft voice
And when harmony joins,
It makes the most blissful noise

5. A Day at the Museum

After being in the cold and rain,

It's nice to be inside again.

Recovering from shivers, my face red, raw,

I look around in fascinated awe

For I see, in front of me,

A skeletal dinosaur suspended magnificently.

I see creatures extinct, alive, and dead

All of the information gets stuck in my head.

Overlarge fish, prehistoric presentations,

It is all beyond my great expectations.

There are facts on memory and more,

Endless knowledge and information galore!

The museum is certainly tons of fun,

And I'm sad, yet glad, as I step out into the sun.

6. Leaves

We are the leaves.
You think you know us, but you don't.
We can't ever expect you to truly love us
Because we know you won't.
We lend our lives and our strength,
So many times have we bled,

But the bitter truth remains for evermore
That we are carelessly shed.
Does anyone take us seriously? No.
Our opinions don't matter.
Do they preserve or rake us off?
Well, predominantly the latter.
Time after time, we wait
For one word of comfort, one compliment,
At the end, too late, we realise
How much time, in waiting, was spent.
Who notices that we stand tall
And are unbroken by pressure on ourselves?
People still try, believe us,
To shun how far our plight delves.
You notice now, don't you-
How many trials you simply forgot?
Tough. Now nothing can be done
As we, the leaves, begin to rot.

7. A Little Poetry Problem

As I sit down with a diary
And a pen in my hand,
I think of what to write about,
But it all seems rather bland

Should I write about nature?
A tranquil, truthful rhyme
Or the modern days we live in,
What happens all the time

Maybe a fantasy tale
That gets everyone's attention
Or the scientific world
I could pop in a new invention

I could go even further
Into outer space,
But most of the time, none of this
Seems to fit into place

But suddenly, it clicks,
I start writing with a shout
About the fact that I, as a poet
Don't know what to write about!

8. Time for Pleasure

I was up all night long
Utterly immersed in song
Isn't it amazing…

I awoke early with the dawn
Without so much as a yawn
Isn't it odd…

I felt like a child
My excitement went wild
Isn't it exciting…

I finally added some colour
To a world that couldn't be duller
Isn't it astounding…

My thoughts were unbothered and clear
My heart bursting with good cheer
Isn't it comforting…

Perhaps spending time on what I love
Will give my happiness that little shove
Because it's lovely, what time for pleasure can do.

9. A Song

A Song…
It can dull the senses, or keep them awake
From a person, there's much it can give or take

A Song…
Projecting the joys and sorrows of life
Willing you to live through pain and strife

A Song…
The companion through laughter and tears
A listener with an impact that one holds dear

A Song…
A melody with emotional faces, so many
It can give one hope to a person without any

A Song…
A hardly noticed beauty of nature
Etched in my mind, and every other creature.

10. Unnecessary Complication

If you fancy a friendly chat,
Does someone try to put you off?
And when you try to explain,
Do they just sit and scoff?

When you ask for information,
Do they get into your head
By not coming out clean and specific,
But straying from the topic instead?

Do they get irritable and worked up
Over the most trivial things
And make things unnecessarily complicated
Without considering what cooperation brings?

They might have something going on
So, try to figure it out,
Perhaps quietly and gently;
You don't want them to shout.

Offer a helping hand
But if all attempts are refused,
You can't do a thing about it.
There's a lot, in the end, that they'll lose.

11. Let Down

It's human to expect things
It's human to want not to
It's normal that things don't work out,
That you feel miserable about it, too.
Then, these things fade away
No more do you lose heart
Unless, of course, an intervention
Brings pain right back to the start.
You tell me not to get excited
That I might face disappointment again
I'd be just fine if I hadn't been told
Like a forecast for stormy rain.
Haven't I faced such sorrow too much?
I have told you once too many
Even if in vain, my hope would exist
Because of you, I haven't any.
So, leave me alone, don't bother
Don't let me down even worse still
It hurts more than any nasty shock
This is why I struggle with a beaten will.

12. Remembrance

Well, it's been a while
Since you left us without warning,
But even though you are gone,
I have something to say; a calling.
You always brought along joy and merriment
Good cheer and laughter,
A smile that could lift up spirits
And that would linger long after.
You helped so many people,
Did more than any other,
Amid such serious work,
Always the light and cheery brother.
An incredible person to look up to,
Remaining a part of us all, held dear
The warmth left behind never forgotten
Its dying embers burning right here.

Daydreams

13. Your Words

When the world has turned me inside out
And has never looked more grey,
Your words come rushing through my mind
Suddenly, I have a lot to say.

When I am broken, lost, and confused
And all I can see is black,
Your words come rushing through my mind
Suddenly, I am fighting back.

When I feel like I am nothing
And the pain is hot and white,
Your words come rushing through my mind
Suddenly, I am in hopeful flight.

When I do not know where to go
Because the path ahead is winding,
Your words come rushing through my mind
And my doubt is no longer binding

When I struggle to form words of my own
For reasons I cannot understand,
Your words are whispers in my head
Now my own words are at hand.

When I feel awfully alone
And I'm tired, it's too hard to continue,
Your words are flashing before my eyes
I see in them a friend in disguise
My eyes sparkle, and I cannot remain blue.

14. The Memory of You

The aroma of freshly mown grass
The ease and sweetness of friendships past
Lavender buzzing with bumblebees
Rosemary-scented homeland trees
Nettles, rainclouds and rose thorns
Riverbank sunsets and fields of corn

A windy chill and frosty morning
A nightingale's song and robins calling
The stony pavement and a red brick house
A hill of flowers and a harvest mouse
Like that country marsh that tingled the skin
The memory of you reels me in…

15. Flower Picking

In times of old, the sun was gold
Flowerbeds I made by the tens,
Oh, what I would give, to laugh and to live
To go skipping, flower picking again.

But now I'm here, the meadow is bare
Naught but poison all around,
One daffodil and my heart is fulfilled
Heading off, homeward bound.

In times of old, the wind blew cold
Beginning the Spring anew,
Hard I must strive to feel free, alive
And go flower picking as when I grew.

16. Daisy Chains

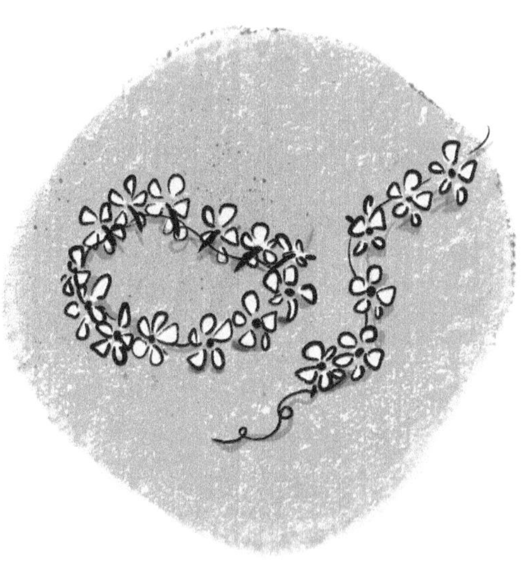

Things were normal as could be
When you would come to play with me
Under the breezy sky of blue
Making daisy chains with you

Light-edged, round, pink, small
A hundred dainty petals would fall
Like our childish faces when we'd laugh
Held up by a leaf-green staff

Now I see them through a lens
And familiar handwriting, hence
Those daisy chains connect us still
For evermore, I'm certain they will.

17. A Good Morning

Nothing feels more certain to a smiling face
Than the morning chill, the gale's embrace
Enthralling it is, the abyss of midnight sky
Alone with naught but stars and a bright eye
The gloomy and dull and beautiful are but one
Never could I choose, but away with blinding sun

18. Cloudy

My eyes fly open, my spirits lift
When I hear an endearing yelp at the window
I rush to it and open it, for your Majesty,
Come plodding in on your soft feet of snow.

You drive that wet little nose and head
Into everybody's jeans,
When we move, you follow, tripping us over
And howling, we know what it means

I serve you your meal, as you like it
Having to shove it in your face,
Yet your Highness looks up expectantly
And searches for it, running all over the place.

You make a mess everywhere,
Cause havoc hard to be ignored,
Oh, but there's something in your face or that fuzzy little tail
That keeps you widely adored.

After bugging us some more,
You steal someone's spot on the couch
Looking for affection, but kneading with your claws,
I can't help but chuckle at the familiar "Ouch!"

Your Grace curls up on my lap
And looks up with those wide, clueless eyes
Being exhausted from purring,
You fall asleep, to no one's surprise.

I gaze upon your dozing form,
A warm blanket of varying hue
In slumber and in waking,
A funny little beacon of love through and through.

Nightmares

19. A Letter to Myself

Please, please forgive me
Tell me what I have done
As long as you hold back
I feel like I have no one
The tears of pain are real enough
Throbbing with their intensity
What will it take for you to be kind?
The torment is killing me.

20. The Fraud

The fraud, the monster who haunts me
Was emerged from an innocent, kind thing
Yet, like a Venus flytrap,
Lured pieces of identity with its cunning grin

A vile creature with a sinister smile,
'Twas a delight but to its victim
It fed on the admiration it got
And the despair of the one it had tricked

A thief it was, nothing more
Stealing parts of your individual soul
What was special about you is its alone
It diminishes a star into a black hole.

21. A Mask

She told me she was happy
Of course, to happiness she was prone
But when she thanked me for everything,
I didn't understand her tone.
I saw her make new friends
And even talk their way,
I thought that it was excellent
And I blindly turned away.
Then, as time went by,
She was still a happy bird
But changes overcame her
To her character, they were absurd.
She was triggered by every comment,
Kept herself under lock and key,
She became all rebellious
But still had fun; good enough for me.
However, years later,
I heard a stifled sob
Followed by faint, heart-wrenching singing;
This was no ordinary job.
I walked into her room
Her eyes were blotchy and red

She was hugging her knees, singing to herself
While crying on her unkempt bed.
Then, she finally told me everything
I felt my jaw drop
As she told me, her woeful hurt
Didn't seem to stop.
She explored much-awaited lands
Hoping to find buried treasure
But, try as she might, sand turned to stone
And she abandoned every measure.
She became encased in rocks
Every time she flung one far,
It landed on her close ones,
Giving them a regretful scar.
Every small, insignificant task
Turned into plentiful stress
So, almost every single day
Was one of deep distress.
She put on a happy face
And succumbed to tears alone-
She only took her mask off
When she was on her own.

22. Enough.

"That's it, you've gone and done it
Pushed me much too far
Who always makes fun of someone's anger?
It's sure to leave a scar
Joke's on you, I'll screech all I want
Then be oblivious to whatever you are."

"Oho, little girl, oh so clever
Difference it shall make not
You shall treat me with respect
Or sit and slowly rot!
After all I've done for you,
In your copybook, yet another blot."

"Little girl?! Not by half
To convenience you mould my age
It is you who make me feel puny
Then expect me to be centre stage
Grown-ups are blind to their own mistakes
And you say I've no right to rage?!"

"Humph! Dear child, when you've seen
As much of life as I
You shall accept the truth in my words
And see it is futile that you cry
Others can go off, for all I care,
It is age that wisdom is measured by."

"Typical, the elderly downplay
The wisdom in the eyes of youth
Although a bit naughty, never haughty
Their spirit killed, seen as uncouth
The only way I'll ever do what you've done
Is if I forget the truth."

23. A Soldier at War

A Soldier stands tall on the battlefield
All poised and ready
In his mind, so does another soldier,
Gun aimed and steady
The Soldier does his best to react calmly
At the enemy's jeers
In his mind, The Other does anything but,
Wounding himself through absence of fear
The Soldier roars and charges
Sending bullets flying all around
In his mind, The Other charges
Fires at himself, and hits the ground
No matter what The Soldier does,
He detests himself for it
In his head, The Other writhes in place
The wounds increasing, bit by bit
The Soldier collapses, lifeless
As the enemy watches behind cover
Both soldiers lay numb, defeated,
Smile and say, "The war is over."

24. The Horror

Many are frightened of darkness, heights,
Ghosts or other figments of horror
It may even be insects, rodents
Or reptiles that inspire terror.
Me, I am bothered
By neither snake nor absence of light;
Actually, I am quite fond
Of things which give others a fright.
The one thing that gives me chills,
An occurrence I utterly loathe and despise
That can leave me in shock and tears
Is causing the disappointment in someone's eyes.

25. Pain

The years grow long and hard
With the ferocity of a cane
Incessantly bringing up past bruises
Stinging and scarlet all over again
But what is there to fret over
When all needs can be fulfilled,
Showered with reason to be light of heart
Why, then, am I not healed?
The bitter truth is everything
Life been forced upon a smile
A person stagnated, stunted and bled
Stowed away in a wicked place
Alone and trapped within the mind
Left to fall and fall… and fall from grace.

26. Life Is a Raincloud

Black.
Why won't it all go black?
Then maybe it won't matter what I lack.
The constant drumming against my brain
Is something I'd leave, and never look back.

Sleep.
Why can't I drift off in sleep?
Every morning, my head lurches and leaps.
The dread washes over my thumping heart
Until I am submerged in terror, neck deep.

Pain.
Why must there always be pain?
Wracking with sobs until I go insane.
Happy or sad or angry, it follows,
Physical, embracing, too much to contain.

Sorrow.
Why surface, my sorrow?
From empathy, from family to borrow.
Once over, a figment, faded and gone,
And will return a hundredfold tomorrow.

Feel.
Why can't I even feel?
For what's going on- nice, awful, real.
Could care less for myself, I'm never there,
Left to writhe in apathetic ordeal.

Forget.
Why do I always forget?
Once I'm happy, all this was fanciful fret.
The horrors come, leave, and haunt until death,
Life is a raincloud; miserable, dripping wet.

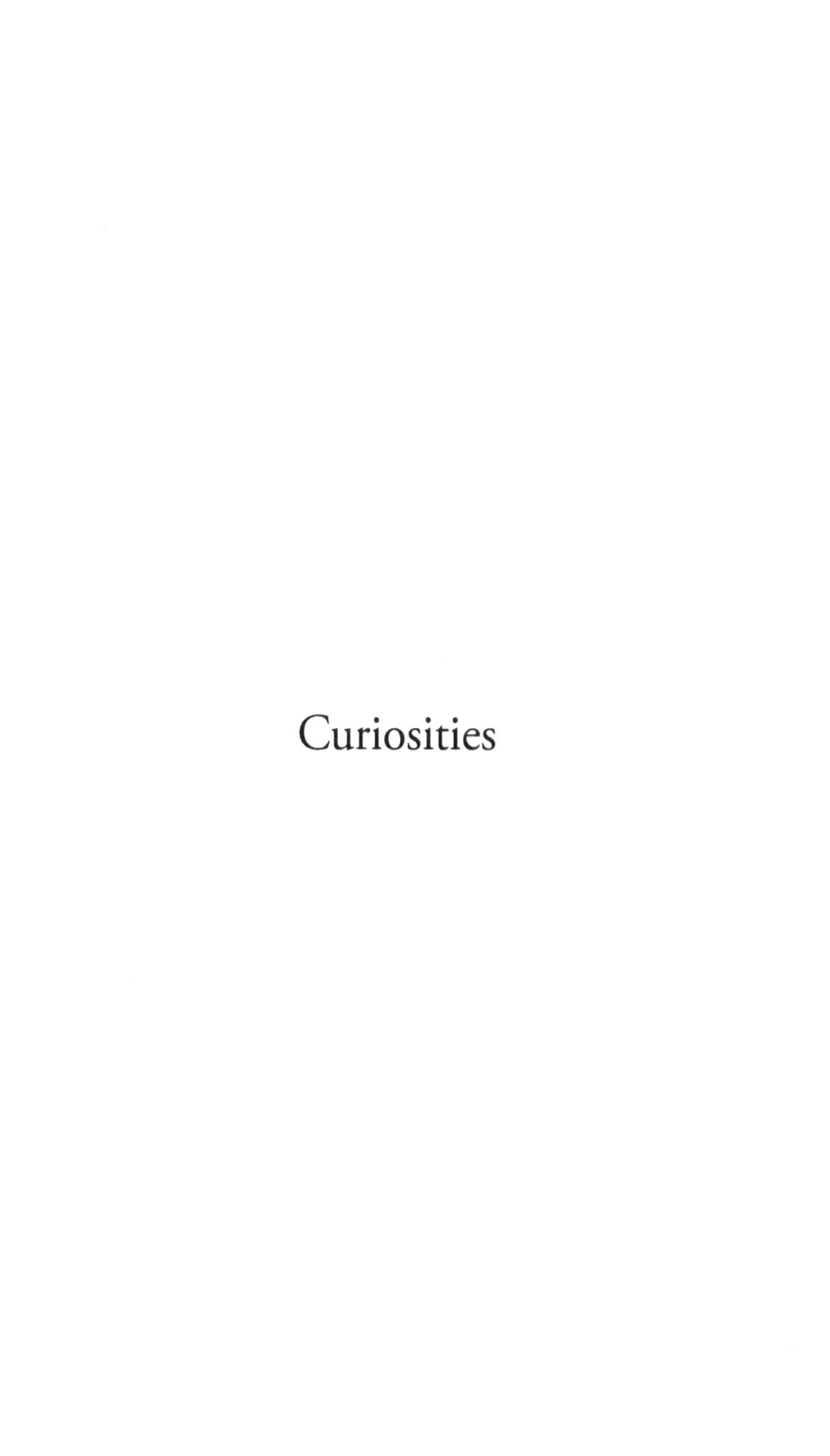

Curiosities

27. Cupboards

If ever I'd go to the theatre,
An unusual thought would ensue
That the actors on stage or on screen
Are more like cupboards than I knew.
Within sits a whole variety of things
Though some may be empty and bare,

Some with colour inside, some filled with decay;
Unsure of exactly what lies in there.
Yet they are mostly appreciated
For a pretty, decorated outside,
Though even the plainest ones
May have wondrous beauty to hide.
Whether sturdy or frail
Each one has talents, at least a few
Anyway, when their doors are shut,
They're impossible to see through.

28. Coffee

Oh, I want to run amok in the house
And skip and jump and twirl
No boring inconveniences, dangerously wide-eyed
My head in an untameable whirl
The deadly flame of work I'll douse
Concentration diminished, all gone
No reading or writing or peace will subside
This bold as brass, carefree rant I'm on
A bit too much caffeine will arouse
The habit of saying words again and again
No other way could any 'grown up' world provide
The mind of a child, free of refrain

29. Insomnia

Everything dark and hidden away
Touched by soft blue light
Wide awake to see it,
There will be no sleep tonight
Trial without success
Behind desperately closed eyes

Torture, head pounding,
The feeling intensifies
Naught but music exists,
Echoing in the chamber, so dark
Emptiness engulfing it all,
Memories begin to spark
A lonely white candle
Ablaze in the cold, dark room,
Nothing to do but ponder,
And await the morning gloom
As dawn silently approaches,
Blue moonbeams sadly fade away
Beautiful, terrible insomnia whispers goodbye
To drift farther from memory each day…

30. Frustration

An unfortunately common and frustrating trend
Is that, whether alone or with a good friend,
While standing in a queue
There's nothing fun to do
Especially if it lasts for hours on end.

31. Time Passes

It's scary, how fast time passes
You can barely stop to look
Changes come, rapidly binding
Another chapter of your book…
It's scary, how fast time passes
Followed by every mistake
Never do you know what hits you
As fast as guitar strings break.

32. The Disgustingly Orange Plastic Excuse of a Guitar

Arising with the approaching dawn,
In the dark, empty tranquility, I let out a yawn.
Content with the grey morning, characteristically bleak,
Throughout the stagnant air rings a piercing shriek.

Swerving in my tracks, searching for the noise
That kills all manner of stability and poise,
My seething eyes settle, with enough rage in stock
To throttle my brother's screeching alarm clock.

Shaped as a disgustingly orange plastic guitar,
Making the least sweet-sounding ruckus by far,
Its infuriating trill can only, very smugly,
Wake up the lightest sleeper on Earth- me!

Sinister arm to arm, that wailing alarm
Serves the sole purpose of causing me fuming, internal harm.
I hope it meets a satisfying end, the abominable blister,
Much beloved by its owner, deeply loathed by his sister.

33. Befuddlement

Reciting your flow of thought
Is called thinking out loud,
Of yourself, it's a sin
While of others, you can be proud.
Many credit supernatural belief
For when they come out on top,
But when others say it's luck,
To defend their own hard work, they won't stop.
'To ponder' means 'to consider carefully'
'Ponderous' is 'moving slowly', it's a fact,
Pomp is lovely, pompousness isn't,
Honestly, what good is that?
Pencil graphite is known as lead,
Ignorance is bliss,
I swear, one day I'll lose my head
Over confounding conundrums like this.

Friends and Foes

34. A Way to Fight

Argument was not made to serve the purpose

Of tearing people apart

Rather, a way to fight for causes

That are clutching at your heart.

35. The Raindrop in an April Shower

Fresh as a raindrop in an April shower,
Dainty as a tulip from her home far away,
Elegant as a reed bending in the wind,
Fluttering, a fairy

Gentle, adventurous, strong.
Although irk each other we did,
We also danced, we also laughed together,
How I longed to reach her shore,
But I could not
And envy kindled.
Yet the tide could not wash away admiration
Of how she lives, with vibrance and grace
To she who has everything I lost,
You are truly brilliant
A shimmering star.

36. Moonbeam

You gave us love from the bottom of your heart,
You filled our lives with talent and art.
To have met you, it was a pleasure
Our memories shall be treasured
I wish we didn't have to be apart.
We look at the moon and see your face
Among the shining stars in space.
I would cross the whole galaxy
Just to play our symphony,
Thus would begin the great chase.
When we are run through with the knife
Of pain, helplessness and strife,
I think of your smile,
Stare at our pictures for a while,
And continue trying to get on with life.
It is guaranteed that there will never be an end
To the light we share and try to mend.
Although across ocean and sea,
You'll always be with me,
A wonderful, undoubted, true friend.

37. My Biggest Mistake

Back when you were yourself,
You were honest, sweet and kind
Your later influences should have been better
Because you left all that behind.
I would be shocked if you cared about
Anyone but yourself now
Yet you are sly enough to fool me
Make me forget your true nature, somehow
A happy smile adorned your face
Only to be replaced with a sneer
Whenever misfortune arises,
You delight in taunting whoever is near.
However, you get sad, you cry
The truth does hurt, doesn't it?
And I, being who I am, afraid to hurt others,
Feel guilty with the force of being hit.
When we were younger, I protected you
I got furious when you were brought pain,
But for naught, since now you tell me I do not care
And to leave with utter disdain.
You must be right about everything
Enter the logical fallacies

You cheat, and when you have been beaten,
Are you honest? Oh, please!
As if you care about my feelings
Putting all my faults on show,
Then you are deaf to the pain in my voice
When I truthfully say, "I know."
If something bad happens
It is always caused by 'me',
You point out all my fake mistakes
It's sick, it brings you glee.
Enough, now here is one from me
Yes, I have thought this through
You want my mistakes? You just got lucky,
My biggest mistake was considering you.

38. Recurring Regret

An irritating brother
A stumble in action
For a second, I see him fume,
A downpour of harsh words
Painful blows, then he goes
And I retire remorsefully to my room.

39. Dear Brother

Okay, you're right, I'm rarely nice to you
To me, you're an annoying little stinker,
But maybe, there's a reason
You see, you're such a voracious thinker
You pick one thing, I pick another
Since we're so fixated on each,
We're focused on complete opposites
Every disagreement is a personal breach.
We can go in any direction together
And forget it every time
But when we do, I couldn't feel blue,
Our existences mutually less of a crime
So, let's spend time together,
Bond over what we love, more than ever
Alas, no matter what, we shall always continue
Our mutually annoying endeavours.

40. When I Met You

When I moved country
I doubted I would come through,
It was like an aliens' planet
Until I met you.
Everything I loved drifted away
My heart's desire withdrew,
For years I sat in misery
Until I met you.
I did things for the sake of it
Lost people I thought I knew,
I forgot who I was and cried a flood
Until I met you.
Now that old ills have left me
It feels too good to be true,
I can look forward to something special
All because I met you.

41. My Direction

You ask, I answer
Why do you still ask?
Have I not repeated myself so?

I answer, you question
Why do you doubt my reason?
Is my word not good enough to go?

If, when I answer
You cannot hear me,
Flying in comes the reprimand

If I must wait
To best express my words,
You feel I have ignored your demand

When I do not seek guidance
Why do you try to guide me?
Can't I go in my own direction?

I'll lose my way, and find it again
As myself, with my own thoughts;
I am no one's little resurrection.

Stories

42. A Voice from the Past

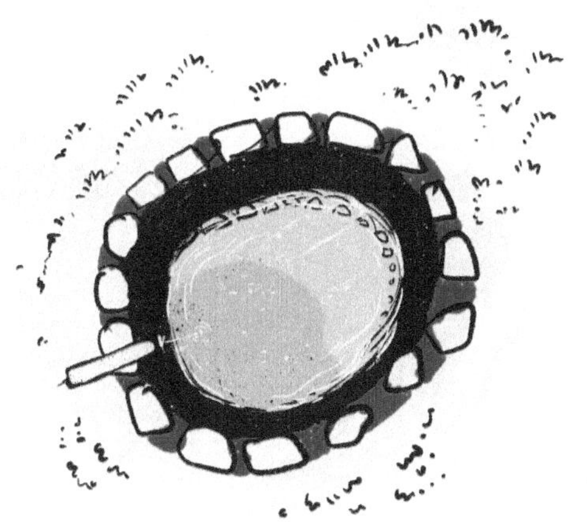

A voice from the past whispers
As gentle as falling snow
As beautiful as a frosty morning
Alight with a silver glow.

A voice from the past echoes
Warm as Autumn leaves fluttering below
As soft as a Fall morning
Alight with a golden glow.

Enchanting and alluring, too much so
Deep as a well whose bottom does not show
To stumble and plunge in could mean becoming lost forever
Whether fate allows resurfacing, you never know.

43. Great Big Burden of Months

I had set off on a journey at sea
From a small port city, dear and sturdy
I still wonder, time after time
Whether the sight of it will ever again come before me.

Battling the tumultuous, stoic tide
While chasing the ever-elusive foe,
Patience, haste and warning
Were prevalent thoughts in which the subconscious did confide.
But to end in so abrupt a way
After such embellishment of adventure
Acceptance was the lesson of that tragic storm
I returned ashore, maybe to turn back another day.

44. Perseverance

Although the days pass in pain
Any thought to pursue tasks largely in vain
The bleak, empty hours
Amid April showers
Won't last just for time to be slain.

Though blank spaces do remain swift
And each moment in time is a gift
You need not fret
Over empty hours spent
For the world is now caught in a rift.

Indeed, hard ages, on they drag
Smiling sunbeams suffer, faces sag
Let not the heart be stilled
Even by that which kills
As the moon still shines, a stolid, scarred flag.

Each daffodil, each bird or beast
To bloom and grow, it never ceased
Endure you must
Choking clouds of dust
From our struggling bonds to be released.

45. Stranded

A long-isolated dream and I
Hazy, all but forgotten
Collided so hard,
It knocked the wind out of me
Leaving me lonely and volatile
In tremulous fury often

Embedded by a shard
Drenched in pain and misery

46. Oasis

That vivid, vibrant dream
Was really you, your past
A happy one for certain
Even though it didn't last
But your life is continuous
Don't give up, calmly carry on
For you create your future
And these difficult days will be gone

47. Worrying Away

A gleam appears in her soft eye
She leaves all the chatter
Feet like the rain patter
Slight, a hunched figure in black, shy
Needles raking her throat, bone dry
Worrying her way to Wistful Lake

Reeds swaying in the wind
Oh, the actions to rescind
The willows' weeping to partake
Their sheltering boughs never shall break.
"Here I shall remain, till I wither
The dawn, the calm
Their comforting arm
My mind and heart are in such a dither
Eyes like two overflowing rivers
Perhaps to look back and ponder
The revelries I've seen
What has and might have been
Then worrying my way over yonder."
To remain without pain in wistful wonder.

48. The Pages of Yesterday

Flipping through the pages of yesterday,
I gaze in dumbstruck awe
At the proof of what I used to think,
I heard, felt, and saw.
Was that wide-eyed creature really me—
The one who skipped happily to school,

Who never knew a moment of self-consciousness
And was sometimes a perfect fool?
A fairy whose world has no magic left,
A ballerina whose balance is now gone,
A performer who developed anxiety
Hard to say the imagination and wonder live on.
Yet with every new page
Come new memories and thrill
Alas, I can never expect the future to be easy
Because it never will.

All I can do is sit by a window
Remembering what the pages of yesterday hold
Hope for a better tomorrow, carry on with today
Trust and move on as the chapter unfolds…

49. The Drill

Walking, skipping, running away
Through flourishing forest and land of decay
Elbowing through crowds, a lone castaway
Wind whipping past, but never once led astray
Hopping over shining stones, running still
Galloping amid flowers, not one tear to spill

Nothing to lean on, neither wall nor windowsill
Only light feet to run far from the drill
Alas, to reach a thicket, too sharp to make the trip
Brambles with lurking doom in just one slip
Screeching to a halt, slowly losing grip
Glistening eyes watch the drill, an advancing pirate ship
Now no open fields, just a desk and walls four
The world takes the wings with which you used to soar
Sitting with a hole the drill made long before
Youth and magic tragically lost forevermore.

50. The Song of Joy

One for the richness of shouting
Two for the raging show,
Three for the knocking unsteady
And back to dark recesses I go

My song is one without pouting
I glide through a golden flow,
To rush like a river, always ready
And ebb away nice and slow

But I am forced to hide, wishing
For one day not to feel hollow,
To feel, quite simply, happy
To burn, to flicker, to glow.

51. The Sea

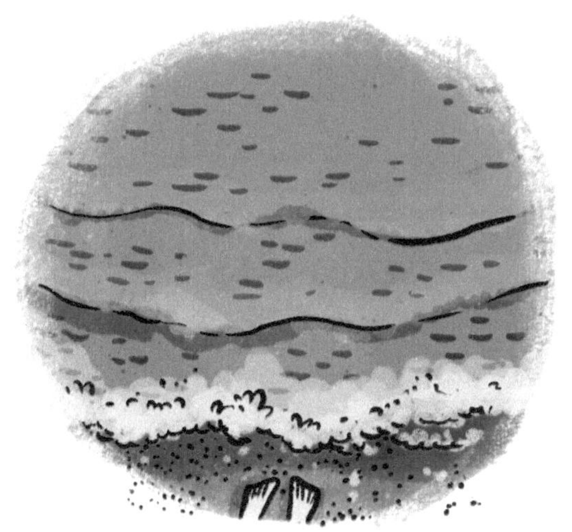

The winds are high as the tide sets in
Hue changes in the sand,
A warning cry from gulls within
This haven in a perilous land.
For when is peril ever more great
Than when the very ground shifts beneath,

Waves make misery never more than sheathed hate
Crashing on the shore, and shattered, bequeath
Tenderness following unhindered rage
Warmth of the merry sun on water,
Uncertainty that rosy silhouettes are a true visage
Does life thrive or cower by the storm's daughter?
Yet my unending ocean is there to stay
Unlike that haven shore, slowly washed away.